THE BUZZARDS' ROOST
AND OTHER POEMS

Copyright © Beasley Leffew 2015

All rights reserved.
No part of this publication may be reproduced, distributed,
or transmitted in any form or by any means, including photocopying,
recording, or other electronic or mechanical methods, without the prior
written permission of the publisher, except in the case of brief quotations embodied in critical reviews and certain other noncommercial uses
permitted by copyright law.

Book design by Leif Södergren

Cover photo by Sarah J. Smith

Back cover photos by author

ISBN
978-91-982015-7-4

contact:
buzzardpress@yahoo.com

BUZZARDROOSTPRESS
Bloomington

THE BUZZARDS' ROOST
AND OTHER POEMS

BEASLEY LEFFEW

CONTENTS

KENTUCKY

3 THE BUZZARDS' ROOST
4 GHOST FARM
7 CIRCE IN SIMPSON COUNTY
8 ON LICK CREEK (1950)
11 AT THE TOBACCO AUCTION
12 HILLSDALE, SIMPSON COUNTY, KENTUCKY
16 IN MEMORIAM
19 NEW MOON

SEASONS

23 WINTER SOLSTICE
25 CHRISTMAS DAY 2014
26 THE ICE FISHERS
28 THREE HUMANIST EASTER POEMS

INNER SPACES

- 34 WHAT IS REAL
- 36 LE CERCLE SPORTIF
- 37 BIRTHDAY
- 38 L'HEURE BLEUE
- 40 LOONS AT BOUNDARY POINT
- 42 INSIDE OUT
- 43 À LA RECHERCHE DU TEMPS PERDU
- 44 A GREEN BOUGH
- 45 REUNION
- 46 BIG SUR 1969
- 49 HOW I GOT HERE

NOTES IN PASSING

- 53 CAN WE TALK?
- 54 MONTAIGNE'S CAT
- 56 POOLSIDE AT THE SINGLES' APARTMENT
- 57 IN THE OLD PEOPLE'S HOME
- 58 FISHING FOR WORDS
- 59 VILLANELLE: ENTROPY
- 60 RONDEAU: YARD SALE
- 60 TANKA: AT THE BALLPARK
- 61 READING GARCIA LORCA
- 62 PHOTOS AND ILLUSTRATIONS

KENTUCKY

KENTUCKY

THE BUZZARDS' ROOST

On Saturdays the families came to town.
The women did their shopping for the week;
The men would go, first, to the barber shop,
As much for conversation as for trims.

Then later on, and one by one, they'd drift
Up to the courthouse square, and light upon
The benches on the eastern side; from there
They'd while away the murmuring afternoon.

They joked and gossiped, traded pocket knives.
They used their knives to shave thin graceful lengths
Of fragrant cedar, ivory smooth, to give
Their hands, unused to rest, something to do.

The cedar ribbons from their whittling sticks,
As fine and curled as any milliner's,
And scented silkily as fine perfume,
Would pile in pillowy nests beneath their seats.

"I see the Buzzards' Roost is full today,"
My Dad would grin,"They look for all the world
Like they'll be roosting permanently there."
And so they are; for with their pocket knives

And whittled sticks they carved a memory
Of innocence and peace. And now, years since,
A breeze at blue twilight will bring the scent
Of cedar shavings from a vanished day.

GHOST FARM
SIMPSON COUNTY, KENTUCKY

It was a spooky place, Grandfather's farm.
At night, around a corner of the house,
One sometimes heard the muffled tramp of soldiers,
The ghosts of Forrest's men, to Shiloh bound.

And late on Springtime afternoons appeared
Their campfires' smoke arising from his fields.
At twilight, at the darkling forest's edge,
A phantom figure would appear, waiting.

Strange hovering lights and floating orbs were seen
About the caves and sinkholes on the farm.
One night a fireball raced across the porch,
Arousing speculation more than fear:

"This goddam place is haunted," Uncle said.
"It's more a kind of grace," Granddad replied.
"The spirits feel a comfort on my land."
"Well they're the only ones," my Uncle said.

But as a child, I felt a comfort there,
And nursed the hope a spirit would come to me,
Come rising with the mist from off the fields,
Or from the stones I found, deep in the woods.

Returning to those woods decades later,
I found, within a glade, a ring of stones
Still there, where I had placed each one of them
One summer's day. I still recall the light

And how it filtered through the forest gloom,
An immemorial light, as alien,
As strange as funerals, or circus clowns.
Alone within that secret timeless glade

I felt that I would suddenly dissolve,
Would disappear into some strange unknown;
Perhaps into this ring of stones, become
A crystal in a dark and silent dome

Or else dissolve into the weightless light:
A phantom at forever's edge, waiting.

KENTUCKY

CIRCE IN SIMPSON COUNTY

"This little pig?
Oh, he used to be an unruly
Boy with bad manners.
So I changed him.
He's much nicer as a pig."

Because I believed her,
I didn't dare
           ask about
                      the dog.

ON LICK CREEK (1950)

My aunts have brought their washing to the creek.
The three of them each raise their skirts and wade
Into the shallows, where in rainbow'd spray
They do their weekly linen laundering.

I sit beside a rippling rapids, where
In dappled darting shadows I have made
A little corn-husk boat, and in my boat
I place my unsuspecting aunts, and send

Them thrilling o'er the rapids, down the creek.
Their bright red hair is blazing in the sun,
Like streaming flames that lick my fragile craft.
They laugh and sing out to the Mississippi,

And then they sail down to New Orleans, where
They boldly flash their skirts above their knees,
Dance mad fandangos in a Creole hall
With black musicians from the vieux carré.

And just before the dawn, their raucous laugh
Echos up to the moon o'er Jackson Square
Where General Jackson, on his prancing steed,
Lifts his hat to them, admiringly.

An echo from the moon, I hear them call
"Hey, Mister Daydreamer! It's time to go!"
They gather up their wash. They act as though
It's just another ordinary day.

But I know where they've been.
Their secret's safe with me.

KENTUCKY

AT THE TOBACCO AUCTION

He placed his child atop the burley stack,
His way of saying to the buyers there
He had a family at home to feed.

A season's sweat he's put upon the block,
The careful cultivation of the crop
Through summer's scorching heat and autumn's frost

The sweltering barn, the freezing stripping-room,
And bundling every leaf into the hands
That rustle like the skirts of dancing girls.

It all comes down to this: A single word -
A shouted "Sold!" declares the auctioneer.
Another year of life and labor done.

His worry and his work brought this reward:
A few bills paid, a wife's new dress for church,
A pair of children's shoes, new overalls,

Hard candy and an orange on Christmas morn.

HILLSDALE
SIMPSON COUNTY, KENTUCKY

I. The Store

The store's abandoned now, but long it stood
Beside the dusty road that led from town,
Its nearest competitors ten miles away.
It was remote, but thriving, serving as
Commercial center as well as gathering place,
It served its clientele with needed things:
Canned goods and staples, sacks of flour from which,
The contents baked into a wagonload
Of biscuits, then the sacks themselves were made
By careful, thrifty farmwife hands into
Skirts and shirts the family would wear.

Inside, the store was lit in dusty haze,
A sort of fuzzy gloom; its shadowed shelves
Held cans and bolts of cloth, jarred jelly beans,
Hard candy, and upon request, there were
Baloney sandwiches for the working men
Who took this lunch back to the fields, or else
They ate together on the store's front porch.

The store's proprietor would often give
Credit for these necessary goods
Against the time when all the crops were sold,
And when the dust of harvest settled down,
Accounts would all be settled, the books marked paid.

The store stands now an empty echoed shell;
Its shelves hold only dust, and in the moted air
There can be heard the country-cadenced voices
From the church nearby, a gospel memory
Much like the store itself, for it is now
A sepia memory, one lost to time.

II. The Church

The sacred and the secular, they stand
Close by each other, separated by
A dusty path that leads between the store
And the church, that portal at the edge
Of what may lie beyond. It may be said
That here is commerce of a different type:
Instead of beans and seeds the store affords,
What's offered here for sale's eternal life,
Salvation and, for those who will believe,
A heavenly home, the price of entrance paid
By Christ himself. The customers await
The final tallying of their debts in life,
And trust the great Pardoner will find
Accounts in order, and the books marked clean.

Inside the dim recesses of the church
Are dusty ferns upon the window sills
And tattered hymnals that contain the songs
That generations of this fellowship
Have hymned their way through countless Sunday morns.
    Amazing grace, how sweet the sound
    Dust thou art
    That saved a wretch
    To dust returneth
    Like me.

KENTUCKY

III.
The Cemetery

As Elisha, my grandad, was being lowered
Into the earth, one of his daughters screamed,
Ran forward to the yawning pit and there
She flung herself onto the dusty ground.
We thought that she was overcome with grief.
There was that, but it was something more:
For she was terrified, and afterward
She divulged a vision she had seen:

Rising from the grave a wall of flame,
Great licking columns of the bluest fire
Ascending high into the staring sky.
This apparition had within its midst
A mighty light, bright shining as the sun.
Nobody else had seen this ghostly thing.
It was dismissed as pure hysteria;
And yet Elisha was the seventh son
Of a seventh son; always there was
A mythic strangeness that surrounded him.
I like to think it was his prophet spirit
That rose that day upon the bluest flames
Into the staring sky above his grave.
Dust thou art,
To dust returneth.

And so he joined the rest, all of them kin
In one way or another, citizens
Of this silent hamlet that survives the world
Of stores and churches that they left behind.
Their crops all in, debts to the store all paid,
Debts to the church redeemed, they are together
In community, beneath the indifferent sky,
At rest beneath the earth they tilled in life,
All gathered for eternity, they lie
Beside a dusty road at Hillsdale Church.

IN MEMORIAM
For Jack Wilz

"Blessed are the pure in heart: for they shall see God."
                                  Matthew 5:8

The day we took our leave, he clasped my hand,
And with his kindly smile, he said to me,
"God bless you." And, skeptic though I am,
I felt a kind of grace had been bestowed.

A little box of polished stone, well made,
One that belonged to him, was given me;
It has a relic resonance, this gift,
Because at times his glance would rest upon it,

His hand would reach to raise its polished lid,
As mine does now: I find within its depth
The memory of those parting words
Echoing from the other side of now.

His simple blessing, from so pure a heart,
The grace his parting words had placed on me,
Means more to me than all the pious prayers
Of all the priests in all of Christendom.

Oh may there be within my heretic heart
Some measure of the purity of his.

KENTUCKY

NEW MOON

My Uncle Benton Gore once had this chair,
A broken-down affair, its leather seat
Worn and cracked with years of rugged wear;
A broken rocker made its ruin complete.

And yet my father fancied this old wreck,
For reasons I could only best surmise.
Perhaps it was a kind of odd respect
For something that, so roughly used, survived.

My Dad said, "Benton, I know you're a busy man,
But if you ever take the time to die,
Maybe you'd leave that chair to me, if you can."
My uncle, smiling, made his droll reply:

"Why, Floyd, that wreck is hardly worth the wait.
I'm only ninety years along, you know.
Be years before I reach the pearly gates.
You'd better take it with you when you go."

And so my Dad and I, our visit done,
And carrying the chair, said our goodbyes.
And soon, our homeward journey just begun,
A drenching rain broke from the night time skies.

We set our heavy load down in the street
And to my wonderment, my Dad sat down,
He settled comfortably into the seat,
And laughed into the rain that swirled around.

He said, "You will remember this some day,
Me rocking in a chair in pouring rain,
Sitting in the darkening roadway
And how we laughed, and then went on again."

The night began to clear, and soon turned fair;
A new moon shone through clouds that floated by,
A crescent, like the rocker of a chair,
Or like my father's grin, hung in the sky.

Some sixty years have passed since then, and yet
Tonight's new moon's the same old moon as then,
And in its curving crescent there are met
The rocker of a chair, and my Dad's grin.

SEASONS

SEASONS

WINTER SOLSTICE

The call of geese across the frozen lake
Breaks the brittle silence hovering here.
The sun's a shadowed filament, opaque,
An icy glow within a crystal sphere.

On this, the shortest day of the fading year,
I walk through woods of snow and glittered frost.
I contemplate the longest night that's near,
And all my bridges burned and bridges crossed,

And what's been found this year, and what's been lost:
Some dreams that disappeared like drifting snow,
Some hopes that I held close, and some I tossed
Into the whispering wind. I cannot know

What future dreams or other calls there be
Before the longest night envelops me.

SEASONS

CHRISTMAS DAY, 2014

The predawn sky was strung with glistening stars
As wondrous bright as any Bethlehem's,
And through the blazing cold of crystal morn
There came, slowly at first, the cardinals,
More splendid in their feathered finery
Than all the rich-robed Princes of the Church.

Resplendent in the early morning light,
An ornament upon a fir tree bough,
A male sends forth glad tidings of the day:
"What cheer! What cheer!" he calls into the air.
And I rejoice to hear this ancient song,
As sacred as this day that's sanctified
By Nature's grace, and not by any gods
That man creates.

                This perfect day requires
No myths or magic births to make it holy.
It's consecrated by the stars and sun,
By birdsong flung across the frozen air,
By something that is true, and not man-made.

THE ICE FISHERS

From a distance, they are painted figures,
Splashes of color in a landscape by Turner,
The view on a ground of white,
Against a sky by Canaletto.

Kneeling as in prayer over their openings
In the frozen surface of the lake, with hope, or faith,
They look to find their reward in depths
They cannot fathom.

What lies beyond the crystal parapet? Will they draw a life
From the other side of the glistening glass
On which, like supplicants, they kneel?
Gazing into the opening between the worlds,

They see a realm of mystery, whose depths
They cannot fathom.

THREE HUMANIST EASTER POEMS

I.
Maundy Thursday
"I know not the man."
Matthew 26:69-75

We're only human. In our frailty,
We sleep when we should be watchful.
Not learning from this, we sleep again

Through the momentous night,
And wake to the cock's recriminating crow.
Denial, and bitter tears.

We deny the chance for grace
When, like Peter, we act from doubt and fear.
Distancing ourselves from what is true,

We diminish our selves
Until, one day, the person we know not
Stares wordlessly back from the mirror.

Not one among us cannot escape our frailty.
We can only forgive,
And hope to be forgiven.

II.

Easter Eggs
Humpty Dumpty sat on a wall,
Humpty Dumpty had a great fall;
All the king's horses and all the king's men
Couldn't put Humpty together again.
				-trad. nursery rhyme

After church, the hidden eggs,
Symbols of an empty tomb
From which life arises.

But Humpty's a different sort of egg,
With a cautionary tale. His tragic fall
Is symbol of our frailty.

For who among us
Hasn't fallen, and felt broken apart,
The pieces of our lives ungathered,
 All unmended, the broken heart,
When no king's horses, nor any king's men
Could mend the scattered shards?

So little children, as you search
For Easter eggs and treats this day,
Be careful not to trample on

The good things that may come your way
Sometimes hidden, often unbidden;
As you grow, mind how you go.

Consider poor Humpty, whose great fall
Provides a lesson to us all. Because, in the end
There are some things you cannot mend

III.

Resurrection
"Why seek ye the living among the dead?"
Luke 24:5

Faith doesn't question, as Reason must,
And Reason must question dead bodies rising,
Yet also acknowledge a faith in things unseen:

That a rose lies humming beneath Winter's dead earth;
That from out the dead leaf a butterfly will ascend;
That the skeletal trees thrum with unseen life arising.

Hummingbirds will return with Spring;
The sun will rise, as human spirits may, with hope,
And Resurrection's message is one of transformation:

The addict defeats his demons, and is restored to life;
Old hurts are forgiven, restoring friendship to life;
And love lifts up the heart in ascendant joy.

Why seek we the living among the dead?
We're only human.

INNER SPACES

WHAT IS REAL

"Once upon a time, I, Zhuangzi, dreamt I was a butterfly. I was conscious only of my happiness as a butterfly, unaware that I was Zhuangzi. Soon I awakened, and there I was, veritably myself again. Now I do not know whether I was then a man dreaming I was a butterfly, or whether I am now a butterfly, dreaming I am a man"

- Zhuangzi teaching parable

The night after my little dog died,
I dreamed I held her tightly to my chest
And I thought that if I held her tightly enough,
I could bring her from that realm into the waking world.
And when I awoke, there she'd be.

But as I began the journey from that world to this,
She slipped from my arms. And now I wonder,
Reading Zhuangzi, if this was my dream,
Or hers.

LE CERCLE SPORTIF
SAIGON, 1963

Tennis in the afternoon slanting light,
The golden shadows shifting through the dusty palms,
And later, drinks at the zinc bar: the tiled floors,
The ceiling fans swinging lazily overhead
In Le Cercle Sportif, the French officers' club.

I had stumbled out of the tobacco fields of Kentucky
And sailed into a Somerset Maugham novel, in which I,
Fresh off a win on the courts, was the main character
In an impossibly romantic scene, where afterward

Beneath a silver sliver of moon,
I danced with an Asian beauty on a hotel rooftop.
"Do you love me?" she asked. "Of course," I replied,
"Down to the last piaster in my pocket."
Which she took, with a smile and a kiss.

My little ship had sailed fields and seas,
And I was ashore in a newfound land.

BIRTHDAY

I am past the age of certainty,
And at an age where all I know
Is that I know nothing.

I am at an age where I perceive
The years as a rushing wind
Howling headlong from the future,

And flying with cyclone speed into the past.
I reach out my hand to slow its progress,
And find lingering on the wind

That Spring's first birdsong;
The Summer's perfect rose;
Sunlight on a windowsill, and

The way Autumn's air softens the light
On evergreen boughs; the scent of leaves,
The silence of a snowfall, long vanished.

Shadows on a wall;
The wind whispering through pines;
A moonlight path across the sea.

Such moments are what remain
Of thistledown years on the rushing wind.

L'HEURE BLEUE

L'heure bleue, the French call it,
That velvet pause that's neither light nor dark,
When the sun in westward flight
Has pushed the day past horizon's glowing edge.

Across the Seine, across the sea and continents,
The enfolding dusk follows, lapis melting into indigo,
The mood fragile as silence, as thin as mist
Falling like memory into this deep twilight.

Sit quietly. Close your eyes. Listen . . .
There echo soft voices in a darkened room,
Answers that came too late,
The foolish dreams, the long goodbye:

Oh be wary of the Blue Hour;
It sweetly summons memory
And trails in its darkling wake
A Seine of tears.

LOONS AT BOUNDARY POINT

A wild and sudden rush of wings, and then
Upon a laboring stream of beaten air
The loons lift up from water's grasp, and there
In circling flight, begin a long glide in

To settle once again, and rest once more
Upon the surface of the darkling lake.
The calm and mirrored surface duplicates
The sky and shadowed trees along the shore.

It is a strange reflection, this, that seems
To make this duplicated scene the real.
The looking-glass itself will not reveal
If I behold what's actual or a dream.

I've often placed my fairest hopes upon
Illusions and mirages such as this.
And in this foolish faith I was remiss,
Remembering where these fairest hopes have gone,

Dissolving as the loon's strange floating cry
Across the lake, into the star-flung sky.

INSIDE OUT

O wad some Power the giftie gie us
To see ourselves as ithers see us!
  ---Robert Burns, from To A Louse

I've lived my life from inside looking out,
And think I know the person that is me.
And yet I've come to form this nagging doubt
I'm not the selfsame person others see.

May I rely upon my inward view
Of who I am, or who I mean to be?
Or do the thoughts of others paint more true
A picture of the person that is me?

There are as many Me's as are perceived
By others who may think me great or small;
And I am by my own self well deceived
If who I think I am is not me at all.

If we could see ourselves through other's eyes,
Would we see anyone we'd recognize?

À LA RECHERCHE DU TEMPS PERDU

If Proust was right, and all it takes
Is a madeleine, for heavens' sakes,
I'll rush right down to the bakery store
And buy myself a dozen more.

Or maybe two. And hang the cost-
Small price to pay to find time lost.
I'll gobble them up, each one, and then
Sit back and wait for my trip to begin.

Wired on sugar, I'll search through the years
And come upon - what - mistakes and tears?
Hmmm. On second thought, what is it
I could possibly gain from such a visit?

So I think I'll skip those magic cakes
And save myself a stomach ache,
And save myself some heartaches, too,
And let lost time remain perdu.

A GREEN BOUGH

*"If I keep a green bough in my heart,
A singing bird will come."*
                        Chinese Proverb

The courtship of the cardinal is delicate:
The male will take a seed and place it
Gently in his lady's beak, and she
Accepts, with what looks like pleasure.

Each Spring brings this renewal of vows
Sealed with a seed. I like to think
It's more than Nature's imperative,
More than a mating urge, lovely though that is -

I like to think it is something like love, an urging
Of the wild heart that throbs in joyous song.
May I keep within my own heart
A space that holds a greenwood bough

And may a cardinal or two fly in
And fill that space with song and simple grace.

REUNION

It wasn't old girlfriends I hoped to find,
Or other old friends that used to be,
But the ghost of a boy that I left behind
The one that dwelt in the back of my mind;
The once and future lad that was me.

"My late bloomer," his mother said;
His teachers' views were much the same.
They could not know inside his head
Were stars and dreams and poems he'd read,
The wind from the future whispering his name.

In the slow unfolding of the years,
The stars grew dimmer, the dreams more faded.
He mixed his laughter with grown-up tears,
Learned what to trust, and what to fear,
Grew a little wiser, and a little jaded,

Became the I that was He,
His unimaginable Me.

BIG SUR 1969

Thirty years old, but still just a boy,
This tsunami of a woman caught him
In a riptide, drowned him in her body,
Choked him with an unquenchable thirst,
Tossed him wildly upon a sea of desire
And cast them both exhausted onto a sun-drenched beach.

Big Sur - where they swam naked with the otters
And the diamonds strewn on the sea
Entered his bloodstream, his heart,
Coursing through his body until he glowed
A new constellation, a man reborn as brightness.

They lighted his way
As he chased this memory, this profligate love
Down all the long years until, exhausted,
He succumbed to a wave of recognition
That what he had called love was passion
That could survive only in retrospect

And he and she became two people he once knew,
Whose story he thinks he remembers.

THE BUZZARDS' ROOST AND OTHER POEMS

INNER SPACES

HOW I GOT HERE

I had no plan in mind for this journey.
No destination showed itself to be
The place my wanderings should carry me.

I had no goal in mind, no grand desire
To make my mark, to set the world on fire
With my achievements, nor to fame aspire.

Left mostly on my own, I groped my way
In fits and starts. At times I could not say
Just what I had in mind, or where I may

Even want to be. At times I stumbled,
Blind to what I should have seen, and, humbled
By my ignorance, I later fumbled

My way back to myself, took up again
The winding path, which often seemed to spin
Beneath my feet. But then there were times when

I least expected it, good fortune came
(Though mostly undeserved). Sometimes the same
Good fortune brought me those who called my name

In love, with care and kindness, helped me see
The way to here. I've sensed, on this journey,
I have not led my life. My life's led me.

NOTES IN PASSING

NOTES IN PASSING

CAN WE TALK?

You'd like to hear from me? How sweet!
I'd like to hear from you.
You know, we could always tweet,
On twitter - that's what I do.

Call you on the telephone?
How quaint, and so old school.
Send an email to your home?
LOL! Uncool.

Meet someplace for a cup of joe,
And have a face to face?
I face to face on Facebook, so
I'll friend you from my place.

Send you a letter in the mail?
That just won't do at all.
U knw vry well that I cn't spell
I'll text you from the mall.

Could we shake hands and just be friends?
I think that would be great,
But my smartphone's molded to my hand.
They'd have to amputate.

MONTAIGNE'S CAT

Monsieur perceived I have a point of view
A lot like humans have, and when he asked
Who is more the pastime when we play,
He or I, "Eh, il depend", I'd say,
Were I to speak the language of Monsieur.

I'd tell him it depends upon my mood:
If I'm inclined to play, then he's the game.
And though he thinks he plays with me, in fact
I play with him. There is a diff'rence here.
Monsieur surmised it well. This caused a fuss.

Monsieur Descartes believed it scandalous,
The thought that I possessed an inner world.
Oh such philosophers! So limited
By arrogance to what they think they know,
They can't conceive a cat's reality.

For how could they, like I, know what it's like
To stare a bird from out its shelt'ring tree?
Or to command a Pharaoh's high regard?
Or to beguile the greatest mind of France
To leave his work because I want to play?

You humans think you master all the world
But I perceive the world to master you:
You do the things you do not want to do
(A cat would never think of doing that),
And you pretend a lot. You would not find

In all the world a cat who would pretend.
Monsieur would ask the question, "How to live?"
"Those who know, don't talk", said wise Lao-Tzu.
If it were not for this admonishment,
And if I talked, I'd answer to Monsieur:

Observe, and don't contend against the world;
Be mindful of the moment that you're in;
Seek quiet and be content with what you have;
And, looking at a cat, or at the world,
Remember that it's looking back at you.

POOLSIDE AT THE SINGLES' APARTMENTS

"I Tiresias, old man with wrinkled dugs
Perceived the scene, and foretold the rest---"
                  T.S. Eliot, The Waste Land

Yon wicked boys with cunning ploys
And stratagems nefarious,
Those saucy girls with tossing curls
And virginity precarious

Do spend the day in aqueous play
And discourse most flirtatious
With secret wiles and comely smiles
And compliments mendacious.

There's lots of skin and pots of sin
That may eventuate.
These satyrs and these sportive nymphs
Will later procreate.

And I, Tiresias, perceive Dionysus
This revelry hath inspired.
I'd like to participate and wantonly dissipate,
But, really, I'm just too tired.

IN THE OLD PEOPLE'S HOME

'. . . a dark wind had been rising toward me from somewhere deep in my future, across years that were still to come, and as it passed, this wind leveled whatever was offered to me at the time, in years no more real than the ones I was living."
                                         -Albert Camus, L'Etranger

A dark wind rising from the future falls,
Insinuates itself beneath the doors;
It glides in whispery tread across the floors,
And sighs in softening silence through the halls.

"You're visiting a penal institute,"
A grizzled geezer tells me as we sit.
"We're doing time for being so damned old."
I laugh at this, but think with grim surmise

A future wind may some day blow myself
Into this company of fading lives.
"Oh, pay no mind to that old poop," I'm told
By a wisp of a lady seated next to me,

"You love it here, don't you, you old fraud?"
"Why, it's a goddamn Borgia court", he says,
"With you old gossips and your scheming ways."
They laugh and wave him off, and breezily

Make him the juicy scandal of the day:
"His walker's parked outside her door at night,"
"And still there sometimes in the morning, too."
They laugh, these spidery old girls, and think,

"More power to him" (privately, of course).
What youthful dreams abide within this place
What memories persist, of love and grace
And sunny days, now long since past, that make

The dark wind that is rising toward them now
A springtime breeze that stirs the blossomed bough.

FISHING FOR WORDS

It's there, that word you're searching for,
Swimming in the ocean of words in your mind,
A minnow of a word that almost breaks the surface
Tantalizingly close, then darts away again.

Slippery as an eel, frustrating as the slipped hook,
It hides in a corner, floating, peering from a crevice
Tempted by your lures; you know it will bite,
Most likely when you least expect it; at midnight, maybe,

It will leap, break to the surface of remembering,
And gratefully, you grasp it. Now that it's yours,
You can let it go, hoping you can catch another.
The word is there; finding it

Is like fishing in a stream of memory,
And catching the one that almost got away.

VILLANELLE: ENTROPY

"Things fall apart; the center cannot hold"
    W.B.Yeats, The Second Coming

Things come apart, and will, in time, decay,
And stealthy Time will work its sly betrayals.
Eventually all things must pass away.

The clock that stops cannot forestall the day
When entropy with sure decline prevails.
Things come apart and will, in time, decay.

As when a levee breaks, there's nought can stay
The forward rushing ruin that Time entails
Eventually all things must pass away.

That word you're reaching for, but cannot say,
Escapes the mind, but vanishing, foretells
Things come apart and will, in time, decay.

As though a wind has blown the word astray,
You chase within your mind its vanished trail.
Eventually all things must pass away.

It startles you to realize the way
Remembrance slows and, in time, it fails.
Things come apart and will, in time, decay.
Must all things eventually pass away?

RONDEAU: YARD SALE

There comes a time for letting go of things -
Cracked crockery and costume jewelry rings,
The glove that made the winning catch that day,
An antique dish, a tarnished silver tray.
The letting go of such odd objects brings

A certain sense of freedom, yet it stings
A bit to put them up for sale; there clings
A sense of final things, and of the way
There comes a time for letting go.

Each object in the yard sale comes with strings,
Invisible connections, with the slings
Of memory held fast, and heavy weighs
The contemplation of the coming days
When age and circumstance conspire to bring
A time for letting go.

TANKA: AT THE BALLPARK

Late innings! The game
Nearly done, and rounding third,
Leaving shouts behind,
A frenzied dash toward home.
Safe! And all covered with dirt.

READING GARCIA LORCA

It's untranslatable, this vision.
The words, the saying, are things we know;
The seeing is what must be surmised.
What Lorca sees is veiled to us; he sees

Beyond language and art, beyond mind;
His reality is a world where longing is green,
Where the cricket speaks in the voice of a child,
Where light shrugs its shoulders like a girl.

It was this world he wished to share, but all
Was crickets' noise, and light that hurt the eyes.
The otherness of nature that he saw
Was threatening, too strange to be endured.

And so, the danger of his pen perceived,
He was shot. The light shrugged, and died.

PHOTOS AND ILLUSTRATIONS

1. "Buzzard's Roost" photo and cover photo by Mrs. Sarah J. Smith (with permission)

2. "Ghost Farm", "Circe in Simpson County", "On Lick Creek", "Le Cercle Sportif", "Reunion", "Hillsdale, Simpson County KY" photos by the Author

3. "At The Tobacco Auction" photo Library of Congress, U.S. Farm Security Administration (Public domain, fair use permitted, no restrictions)

4. "In Memoriam", "Winter Solstice", "What Is Real", "L'Heure Bleue", "Christmas Day, 2014" photos by Leif Södergren

5. "New Moon", "The Ice Fishers", "Loons At Boundary Point", "Big Sur" photos Stock photos from Dreamstime.com (royalty free)

6. "Three Humanist Easter Poems" illustration woodcut by Thayer Carter (by permission)

7. "Inside Out", "Birthday", "Can We Talk?", "Montaigne's Cat", "How I Got Here", "Reading Garcia Lorca" illustrations by Donovan O'Malley (with permission)

8. "Poolside At The Singles' Apartments" photo Stock photos from fotolia.com (royalty free)

9. "Fishing for Words", "Resurrection" photos by Ricardo H. Martines

www.ingramcontent.com/pod-product-compliance
Lightning Source LLC
Chambersburg PA
CBHW060819090426
42738CB00002B/43